APOCALYPSE, DARLING

MACHETE
Joy Castro, Series Editor

APOCALYPSE, DARLING

Barrie Jean Borich

MAD CREEK BOOKS, AN IMPRINT OF
THE OHIO STATE UNIVERSITY PRESS
COLUMBUS

Copyright © 2018 by Barrie Jean Borich.

All rights reserved.

Published by Mad Creek Books, an imprint of The Ohio State University Press.

Library of Congress Cataloging-in-Publication Data

Names: Borich, Barrie Jean, 1959– author.

Title: Apocalypse, darling / by Barrie Jean Borich.

Other titles: Machete.

Description: Columbus : Mad Creek Books, an imprint of The Ohio State University Press, [2018] | Series: Machete | Includes bibliographical references.

Identifiers: LCCN 2017041304 | ISBN 9780814254622 (pbk. ; alk. paper) | ISBN 0814254624 (pbk. ; alk. paper)

Subjects: LCSH: Borich, Barrie Jean, 1959–Homes and haunts. | Borich, Barrie Jean, 1959–Family. | Chicago (Ill.)–Social conditions. | Middle West–Social conditions.

Classification: LCC PS3552.O7529 A66 2018 | DDC 818/.5403–dc23

LC record available at https://lccn.loc.gov/2017041304

Cover design by Nathan Putens

Text design by Juliet Williams

Type set in Palatino and Distro

Cover image and frontispiece photograph by Laurie Migliorino

∞ The paper used in this publication meets the minimum requirements of the American National Standard for Information Sciences–Permanence of Paper for Printed Library Materials. ANSI Z39.48-1992.

9 8 7 6 5 4 3 2 1

For Linnea,
and the beautiful wastelands that made us both.

What are the roots that clutch, what branches grow
Out of this stony rubbish?

—T. S. Eliot, *The Waste Land*

CONTENTS

CONTENTS

PART III: NOTHING WITH NOTHING

PART IV: WHAT THE WATER SAID

PART V: FRAGMENTS AGAINST RUINS

CONTENTS

PART I

MIXING

MEMORY

WITH

DESIRE

WASTELAND OASIS

Indiana 2008

If we were to arrive at this wedding by helicopter here's what we would see. An expanding patch of unnatural green. Neon green. Denial-of-impending-annihilation green. An over-bright amoeba, surrounded by the stacks of Northwest Indiana. Windowless steel mills, smoke spume, ground that appears as if the skin has been scraped away, a rusty, gouged tableau, wasteland gray interrupted by the peacock blue painted exterior of U.S. Steel Gary Works—as if someone in charge had consulted with a home decorating guru. Shall we try blue, Darling? Costume-party, feather-boa blue? Blue to accent these badlands that would stretch all the way to forever, except for the khaki bumper of Lake Michigan.

This decimated plain, punctured by the green of the golf course, is where my father-in-law, age seventy-five, is about to wed his long-lost, newly found, pinkly smiling, high school sweetheart, in the presence of middle-aged children who would not exist if this father, and this mother, had married each other the first time they were in love.

BYWAY, SKYWAY

Illinois/Indiana 2008

Of course we don't arrive by helicopter. Linnea and I fly from Minneapolis to Chicago, then drive the rest of the way to her father's wedding.

The quickest way to get to the communities lining the Indiana Dunes from downtown Chicago is via the byway of the sky. The western entry to the Indiana Toll Road is an elevated highway built on a scaffolding that laces into the far Southeast Side, a steel filigree supporting the highway up and over the old steel workers' city. Even knowing what's ahead, the highway inclining under the wheels of the car as it passes through the toll gate, the signage making clear that this is the exit onto the SKYWAY, it's still not immediately apparent that this is not just a road but a bridge breaking into open air, so then a shock, the way first the old East Side port and then downtown Gary open beneath us, a pictorial centerfold. Gary is a splay of old-century granite stitched together by the steel docks and bridge girders, contained by the jade release of Lake Michigan, cleaner now than when I was a girl, capped by the granulated blue of a mill-punctured sky.

Linnea is driving. I slap her on the shoulder as the Skyway rises over the centerfold. I hadn't expected we'd motor into such familiar and unfamiliar cleaving. We are driving toward a gathering of her side of the family, but driving through the Old Country of mine.

When I was teenager I often ended up on the Skyway by accident, veering onto the wrong exit south from the Loop, usually late at night, my car full of friends, likely drunk or high, when the yellow streetlights cast a dingy pall over the toll bridge gates, suggesting the gateway into Hell or at least Purgatory. Once you enter the Skyway in south Chicago there are no exits until Hammond, Indiana, so those lit-up CHICAGO SKYWAY letters over the toll plaza caused my stomach to tighten. Where am I? Do my friends think I'm a bad driver?

How do I get off, out, home?

By comparison, on this June afternoon, the sky could not be a crisper blue. I could stay in this hanging moment forever, Linnea's steady, square hands clutching the steering wheel, the windows rolled up so as not to muss my shoulder-length hair I'd so carefully flat-ironed in her sister's bathroom, back on the shinier side of the city where we'd spent the night, my chest, overexposed in my low-cut sundress, goose-pimpling in the breeze of the air conditioning, the Skyway incline out and over, the spread of old avenues opening, hail forgotten city, full of grace.

I almost forget we have someplace to be.

HIS NOT DAUGHTER

Minneapolis 1987

I could have gotten out of attending this wedding. In the twenty-two years Linnea and I have been in love, I've never been close to my father-in-law. Linnea hasn't even been that close to him. For our first ten years together, Linnea—the daughter her father had always treated as a son—didn't even tell him about me. He may have been vaguely aware of that woman his firstborn had lived with for some time, but even later, after he declined the invitation to our wedding, he seemed unaware that his oldest had a spouse.

It's his unblinking conservatism which keeps him from full knowledge of all his children but which, in the case of Linnea, takes the form of dismissive homophobia. Genderqueer and male-expressive Linnea, who only wincingly accepts the pronoun "she," is far from a closet case, so her father's dismissal means he's missed a great deal. A dissertation on the evolution of the lesbian novel. Service on the board of a national lesbian, gay, bisexual, and transgender archive. Wearing men's suits to a job as a city college dean. Even in 1987, my leather miniskirt days—when I first fell in love with a suitor in a leather jacket, crisp men's shirts, Western boots—no one could have mistaken Linnea for a conventional man-marrying type of woman. What I first noticed was the way Linnea's jeans fit, tight across the thighs, emphasizing strength—hips that carried the engine of a long stride. Picture Linnea then, stepping across some red-lit bar floor, short curly hair, a big buckle belt, hips cowboy fluid, the posture of the rider, not the ridden, that belt buckle flashing, boots that looked like they were sewn onto the feet, a big brotherly, husbandly, shit-kicking, lover-boy, c'mere-baby bearing that some men wear well, and some butches.

Since everyone knew right away that Linnea and I were seriously in love, I couldn't understand, during those early years, what was keeping Linnea from introducing me to the family father, the way she'd introduced me to the mother, the sisters, the brother, the grandmother, the aunts and uncles, all of them accepting me without question. If Linnea loved me, they loved me, and I was a part of their clan. So what was the deal with Dad?

TROUBLE

Chicago 1985

Before we were officially acquainted, I'd heard stories.

A slight woman with long red hair calls her father from a phone booth in a rough neighborhood, just off the West Side expressway. Her car is parked crookedly along the curb across the avenue, one of those tattered streets in Chicago, by which I mean the flyers and posters stapled to telephone poles, advertising local bar bands or weight loss miracle drugs or ways to make lots of money from home, are torn and ragged, and the paint on the trim of doorways is chipped and the storefronts are shuttered with that accordion-style security fencing that locks down certain commercial districts after dark. Some of the windows are broken and secured by unevenly nailed two-by-four scraps, and the windows that are intact have old blankets or newspaper instead of curtains and nobody is walking around.

The redhead in the phone booth—she's lucky it's one of those phone booths with a working phone—is leaning against the glass, her hair falling forward over her face. This is Linnea's sister, the one who will be a surgeon at the University of Chicago Medical Center. But now she is still in medical school. She is leaning over her open purse, propped up on one knee, and she is digging around for a quarter. These are the days before cell phones, before phone cards even, so it's imperative she find some change. The cigarette-stain-yellow streetlamp catches the red glint in her hair as she finds what she needs, slides the quarter into the slot, and presses the buttons to dial her father's number.

The hood is open on her car parked across the street, not because she's having engine trouble. She's just out of gas, and out of money. Med school is expensive. Her loan money has not come through. She's signaling with the open hood of her car for help, but who will assist her on this shredded, latched-down street in the middle of the night where she's afraid if anyone sees her walking around they'll assume she's in some kind of body business, but not the medical profession? Her narrow figure leaning against the phone booth glass is bright, illuminated like a bone displayed in an exhibit case of the natural history museum. She taps the glass while the phone rings.

She doesn't know yet that eventually she will have to do the only thing she can do, just shove herself out onto the street and walk toward home, and once she does, some friendly cops partial to redheads who glow like bones under yellow lamplight will come to her rescue.

But first she calls her father, the one she's never asked for anything, not even help with medical school. She calls to ask him to wire some money to her checking account, or call a gas station with a credit card, or something, one of those middle-of-the-night rescue efforts only fathers know how to pull off, so she can, somewhere in this lost yellow city, buy enough gas to get her home, to study, to bed. What else can she do but call and wake up her father, and when he says no—says she needs to learn how to manage better, needs to learn how to think about how she spends her money—she will slump harder against the glass, she will raise her fingers to her forehead, and the light glinting off her hair will pierce back into the darkness—a prayer, a panic beacon—which Linnea and I can feel from twenty-five years' distance but which her father still refuses to notice.

BEST MAN

Indiana 2008

To describe this wedding, and through this wedding describe what brought Linnea and me to that precipice hovering over a part of the city I'd long ago left behind, and not only to that precipice but to something bigger, first I need to wonder why the four children of this seventy-five-year-old ultraconservative Swede from the Upper Peninsula of Michigan showed up with their spouses at his Indiana golf course wedding, despite being half-estranged from him for most of their lives.

So I begin to line them up for the wedding day portrait, the way they looked on the occasion of their father's third wedding, starting with the baby brother. He's taller than all of his sisters, taller than his dad, his ruddy arms and back covered in tattoos, hidden today under a navy suit jacket and silk print tie. I notice his full red moustache, his red-and-gray-speckled beard, his sunglasses resting on the top of his head all through the ceremony, even though, as best man, he'll stand up in front of us all, his long red hair pulled back into the ponytail he will eventually cut off and donate to cancer kids, for wigs, as he does every few years. I see a Midwestern hardcore Harley guy, similar to guys anyone who's driven the back roads of the Great Lake states might see riding without helmets down the center of blue highways on

October Sundays. I see too the uncle who likes to tease his young nieces and nephews by threatening to eat bugs and then actually eating them or telling them they have beautiful eyes, have they ever thought of working as eye models?

The kids eventually either laugh or run away screaming, but I've known this guy for over twenty years, since we were all young ourselves, so under all that grizzly bluster I see too a sweet and decent yet vulnerable hero portrayed by the likes of Brad Pitt in the movies, but when I describe him this way to our teenage nieces they squint their eyes and shake their heads at me. What? Harley guy uncle with the steam shovel voice and the bare-breasted, peg-legged hottie chick tattoos? You've gotta be kidding.

PINK LADY

Minneapolis 2008

I started calling her the Pink Lady because she was dressed in pink the day Linnea and I met her, a month before the wedding, six weeks after she'd tracked down Linnea's father, after fifty years, and wound up with a new diamond ring.

The Pink Lady, we would find out soon enough, nearly always wore shades of pink, and pinkness became the way I thought of her. Linnea's father found his Pink Lady, I said, when we told the story to our friends—this tale of lost sweethearts who relocated each other, this lovely lady who chose Linnea's father again, after half a century living with another husband, and the kids and grandchildren of the life she wouldn't have had if she'd stuck with him the first time, or if he'd stuck with her. If any of us, I kept saying to my friends, are alone at age seventy-five, let's hope we find a Pink Lady to love us.

Looking back now I'm not sure the Pink Lady quite knew who I was the first time we talked. She was so sweet, which I mistook for openness to alternatives. Huggy family sentiment is not usually my métier, but I'm also the type who sobs when PFLAG, the Parents and Families of Lesbians and Gays contingent, marches by in the GLBTQ Pride Parade. My crying means LOOK at those families SO accepting they go to MEETINGS. The one time, years ago, that I asked my mom and dad to look into PFLAG they said they were too busy with the Knights of Columbus. That was right after I got my first tattoo, the growling leopard on my right upper arm, which my mother hates and led her then to comment that she'd rather go to a meeting of mothers of daughters with tattoos. She said it with that South Chicago cut in her voice, which she means to be funny, which I've inherited, which then I give right back, the same, twist and cut, when I say, *Mom. The name of that tattoo meeting is PFLAG.*

Which is why, when the Pink Lady, who is the exact same age as my mother, and who reminds me, here and there, of a bustier and more powdered, and, well, pinker version of my mother, sidled up to me and started chattering like a sorority sister, I mistook what seemed to be intimacy for informed sanction. I assumed her new fiancé had already mentioned that his daughter was a lesbian and explained that I was his daughter's wife. It hadn't occurred to me that she was so wound up in her bubble of love that she'd let herself believe the same things waiters and cab drivers assume about Linnea and me, if they look at just form, not content, if they go with the version that makes them most comfortable, me the daughter, Linnea my boyfriend. Or that she'd assume her fiancé had two Minnesota daughters and thank God this one looks like a girl, or that I was simply Linnea's friend or that it didn't matter who I was, it only mattered that I was sitting next to her because she just wanted to talk, pinkly and sweetly about her stumble back into the pink.

She talked as if I'd known her since before her dear husband's death, before the years she spent alone, until her sister insisted it was time she dated again, before all those men had taken her out, some of them rich guys, in those months leading up to finding Linnea's father, every one of them asking her to marry him by the second date. She leaned in then to whisper, as if, through shared experience, I'd understand. *Such a turn-off,* she said, *when they mention marriage already on the second date.*

The trendy café in St. Paul where we'd agreed to meet Linnea's father and the Pink Lady, and the Pink Lady's own middle-aged daughter, Linnea's sudden stepsister who coincidentally lived in Minnesota too, was in itself astounding in the history of our relationship with Linnea's dad. Tea and scones with white chocolate and clotted cream? Sliced French bread with three different varieties of pâté? Linnea and I had never before enjoyed such a lunch with her father. The few times he'd been through town to see Linnea in the past few years, after the ten years of only terse postcards penned in black felt tip, they'd eat lunch in some functional joint, one of those so-called family restaurants that serve coffee by the carafe and eggs any style. Most of the time her dad would pull through Minnesota when it was time to bring his trailer to the dealer in the far suburbs for routine maintenance, during which time Linnea would drive out to meet him, and they'd have a perfunctory lunch before he'd head on back to Michigan. On the rare times he did drive all the way into Minneapolis he never stayed over, never looked me in the face when greeting me, always seemed clearly relieved that I was too busy to come along to eat with them.

I come from brooding, sardonic Eastern Europeans, and the side of Linnea's family that I know best are talk-with-their-hands Italian Americans, so I don't know how to read the pale composure of this stoic North Country Swede. But on this day with the scones I noticed a new lightness. His lips pulled into what, for him, was a smile, his mouth forming a long dash, his cheekbones widening under his silver spectacles. He nibbled on his scone with clotted cream and I wondered if this is what his "really happy" looked like, so strange considering his children all have their mother's burbling-laughter-runneth-from-three-states-over sorts of smiles. Did women of his generation find such stillness an indicator of safety? Or perhaps it's what he whispered in private that made the difference, the pull between hard white silence and some silkier endearment? Words like *I love you, please marry me*, might seem like a lot coming from one who appears he would burst like a sand-filled balloon from the hard drop of too much feeling.

Whatever his trick, it had worked on the Pink Lady. Her bleached hair was carefully disheveled, as if when she dressed she didn't want to appear too eager to see him, and her pink blouse was low cut enough to show off her still healthy cleavage. Her hand shivered when she showed me (a curiously familiar stranger? her new bottle-blond-like-her daughter-in-law?) her ring, a big old flashing rock, and told me oh, she can't believe how excited she is to tell me this story, told me how she found him after all these years, not through the Internet like the young people do but the old-fashioned way—relatives and friends and even the church back in their old hometown in the Upper Peninsula of Michigan, told me that when she finally found him, living just thirty miles from her retirement house in Florida, and long-divorced too, she couldn't believe her good fate, knew right away that something big was happening. And did I know he had a dream about her just a week before she called?

She was still trembling. When she held up her arms they quivered like the shaft of an archer's arrow. I could tell, the way she was talking, that she believed in some higher hand, that she believed love was magic. Maybe she would change him? She was lovely and so pink and smiling so hard she made up for her fiancé's flat grim grin. Her internal quaking caused her new diamond to catch and release the static light of the restaurant, as if the ring were electric, the stone a quiet pink lamp, blinking on and off and on again.

SWEDE IN OUR SHOWER

Minneapolis 1995

A couple times, when dragging his trailer back to Minnesota, the Old Swede followed Linnea back into Minneapolis in order to use our shower. Once he came with the divorcée he was seeing at the time. He'd had a long string of Republican lady widows and divorcées. Linnea told me he'd meet them at the American Legion bar, back up in Michigan or down in Florida. After a few dates his lady friends began making his biannual migrations with him, dragging the trailer back and forth between Michigan and Florida. One of these ladies he'd actually married, but it didn't last long and I never met her.

During one of his brief stints through our city I came home from work to find a strange woman in a prim, pale, buttoned shirt and loose-ratted hair paging through the newspaper at my kitchen table, Linnea making coffee in the stovetop percolator she usually takes down from a top shelf only when my parents are in town, the sound of the shower rumbling from the bathroom that was so oddly placed just off our cupboards. Linnea widened her eyes at me and shrugged. Her father emerged from our bathroom fully clothed and combed—that his white hair was slightly damp was the only evidence of what he'd been doing in there—and he and the woman were gone within the half hour. That was one of his longer visits.

WHAT'S PRESENT IN TIME FUTURE I

Chicago 2015

The future barely contained in this time past is the father who will, in the year following this wedding day, become vulnerable enough to evoke less his children's forgiveness than their sympathy, an adjustment of their view, what's present in time future, the once insurmountable and typically stalwart Swede revealed as another hurt body leaning into wasteland winds, by which I mean his children will find moments, green clearings, in which to embrace him.

But not yet.

ANNIHILATION PENDING

Minneapolis 1988

Linnea and I have an old portrait of us dating back to our first year together, taken at a suburban Sears portrait studio. And as odd as it seems today to think of us going to a canned department store studio to have our picture taken by one of those photographers who specializes in dressing babies up in pirate or pumpkin or fuzzy bunny costumes, that we did such a thing in 1988, before the typical guy working the camera at Sears was likely to have even seen lesbians on TV, is even odder.

We did it because we had a coupon. Because it seemed, then, before anyone outside of gays had heard of gay marriage, slightly wicked to storm the Sears portrait studio in search of a newlywed portrait. Because we were in love and wanted a picture.

Was it the photographer's nerves that composed this unrecognizable portrait of two young lovers with empty eyes? If he was bothered by the lesbians on his stage set, he never let on, so much so that we wondered if he thought Linnea was a man with unusually soft edges. These days we are accustomed to strangers mistaking Linnea for a guy. As she's aged she's lost what few womanly features she once possessed. But then she looked more like a tomboy sort of woman, not uncommon among lesbians, or librarians, or dog school instructors.

Perhaps we were too frightened then to be openly lesbian out-side the city limits, at a mall, in this back room of Sears, and so gave him nothing but blank postures to work with. Or perhaps the pictures are just what they look to be, two lovers reentering the Old Country they'd left behind, where too much is left unspo-ken, where the truth is not revealed, where the shiny gloss is mis-taken for the real, where the annihilation might be pending, but that's OK, we don't notice.

In this photograph, Linnea's hands cradling mine, our gaze is focused on some invisible future, the same God-Bless-Amer-ica place every kid in every yearbook photo is gazing out over, as if we were not in our bodies when the photo was taken, as if we were only our real bodies the way bodies in caskets resemble the long-lost beloved but no longer are the people mourners once actually loved.

I used to tell Linnea—let's take one of the Sears portraits and paste it over a photo of a mushroom cloud. Let's add a dialogue bubble. *Is that the apocalypse, Darling, or are you just happy to see me?*

VISIBLE GRACE, CALUMET

Illinois/Indiana 1950–present

By *apocalypse* I mean my old post-industrial wonderland, the familiar smithereens that run under the Skyway, along Calumet Harbor, between the old East Side ports and Gary, Indiana, and the southeast bottom of Lake Michigan. Always present when I was a girl. I never discussed this wasteland with anyone until, as an adult, I moved away and discovered how the city had imprinted on me.

Not quite the dream wedding locale, the broken granaries with stained outer walls, the unwound skeins of train tracks, the rusty barges, the scrap metal mounds, the dirty water, the russet piles of raw metals, the cylinders and conveyors of the blast furnaces, the peaks of fire torching out the mouths of steel towers.

But also the peacock walls of USS *Gary*. Also, Darling, the undulation of the big lake.

ENTER THE CHAPEL

Indiana 2008

But this was a secular wedding, at the house of the Pink Lady's sister.

Off the Skyway, past the mills, turn where we used to exit, as teenagers, on our way to the Indiana Dunes, but right instead of left.

The golf course is gated, of course. Ornate curlicue gates, built between brick pillars. On either side, long slopes of chemical green lawn. You can't get in without a code.

Unless of course you are the bad element, the unsavory sort gated communities wish to gate against. If this is you, bad guy hoping to strip bare these pretty golf course abodes with their backs turned to the mill smoke, if your wishes are larcenous, don't worry about not knowing the code. Just drive around, over that sloping green grass.

By the time anyone sees your tire tracks on the green, you'll be done doing what you came to do, you'll be gone and the gates will have held.

But our intentions are completely honorable. We just want to be on time for the wedding.

We are punching in a code that doesn't work. We rifle through our papers. What's Pink Lady's sister's name? What's the number? We dial and she picks up. We say who we are and she says WHAT? We tell her again and she says WHAT? She gives us some number. Another code? We punch in the new code and the gate does not open. Cars pile up behind us. Hey, there's Linnea's brother. The Best Man. Wave. Shrug. We call the Pink Lady's sister again. We tell her who we are again, that we are trying to arrive for the wedding. WHAT? We hear the machine tone from her end of the line. She is punching in some numbers. The gate does not open. We hear another jumble of notes, like the tone poem the scientists play for the aliens in *Close Encounters of the Third Kind*. The voice squawks from the tinny gate speaker. WHAT? *I am the groom's daughter,* Linnea says again. *We are trying to come to the wedding.* WHAT? We hear the tones on her end again. Finally the gates swing open, slowly, operatically, the wrought iron curlicues glistening in the sun like flickers from the blast furnaces, as if ushering us into Hell or Paradise.

PART II

IN WHICH

SAD

LIGHT

THE CRUELEST MONTH

Post-Industrial North 2008

April is a cusp—no longer winter, not fully spring, not in the northern American industrial centers at least. When the buds of the few remaining trees of the wasteland swell into greenery, we see contrast. What is the beginning? What is the end? When we see both together, this greening, these bare branches, the burst and the demise, we remember the ways beginnings require endings to exist.

After Linnea and I departed from our first encounter with the Pink Lady, on the drive home from the St. Paul café, we talked about the wedding date, already less than six weeks ahead. I said, *Well maybe this is what it is to fall in love again, especially with someone who knew you when you were young.* I meant to point out the way any of us might feel if we'd stumbled into the budding part of April, the green that is certain to grow.

We've both attended the weddings of young cousins who talk about falling in love this way. They say, *I told my mother—I met the one tonight.* They say, *I knew right way, I'd found my future.* Not just—oh I want to touch her. Not only the kissing, not only the pull to press against someone new, but desire declaring itself as some original feeling, like the memory of how it was before the wounds, before the prairies became the cities, before the dunes were scraped away to make steel. What will it take to bring a wasteland back to bloom?

But this love between Linnea's father and his bride-to-be had already ended, years ago, long before they became the people they'd turned out to be. They'd married others. Now, in what was supposed to be their waning years, they found themselves returned. Or felt as if they'd returned to the start of another, sweeter, arc.

Does such re-encountered sweetness—or illusion of sweetness—heal or hurt?

I wonder if romantic love is a concoction, like the place the early European-American ecologists called the Indiana Dunes Country: once simply part of the Great Lakes glacial terrain, now a commonly held but rarely considered designation for a break in an otherwise wasted territory; a landscape I think I remember, but which in memory transmutes into other landscapes I remember too, but identify wrongly.

And what of a future already serving as the past?

When the Pink Lady held out her hand to show me her engagement ring, it was late April in Minnesota. The way her hand shook, the way she leaned closer to assure me she knew how foolish she must seem, a bride at her age, the way her eyes were shining but unfocused, the way her diamond caught the light—was this dawn or was it twilight? Was she alight or intoxicated? Is love—mine or the Pink Lady's, Linnea's or her father's—an accident, a decision, or just an arrangement we make with hope?

Are these the Dunelands of respite and escape, or is this still just the industrial corridor of Northwest Indiana?

DUNE-ALITY

Indiana 1977

If the word *dune* refers to a vacationland of sand mounded by wind, if the name is more description than history, then the Indiana Dunes at the Lake Michigan shore, down the road from the setting of Linnea's father's wedding, are not quite dunes. People in the region refer to two spots along the eastern lakefront as the Dunes. Warren Dunes State Park, thirty minutes further north and across another state line into Michigan, is the more dune-ish of the two, a margin of sandy knolls, rolling between the parking lot and a shoreline drubbed by freshwater surf. Wind. Beach towels and tanning oils and radios. Sunburn and beer.

The Indiana Dunes are closer in, a half hour back down around the lower bend of Lake Michigan, just a few minutes outside of Gary, not so many wind-sculpted mounds, mostly a flat granular interlude between steel mills and power plants, emissions from the mill stacks smudging what is, further north, a broader, bluer sky. When I was a girl we called this beach *the Dunes* the same way we called open lots in the near South Side industrial suburbs *the Prairie*—not dunes so much as dune-ish-ness, a sandy ecosystem sprung free of the city, a weedy lot uncapped by asphalt, sudden and uncharacteristic space, named for what had been once but was no longer—tall grass prairie, glacier lake dunes. What was long ago trammeled by the imprint of urban industry exists, still, only within the invisible layers of history, and in language. We call things by the names of that which we've taken away.

Here's how to experience the Indiana Dunes as if it really were Vacationland. Stand on the beach, at attention, directly facing the water, arms held out toward the horizon, bent at the elbows, as if measuring the width of a window frame. Spread your palms flat, to form blinders, blocking out the borders of the beach, so you can't see, to the north and to the south, the sulk of smoking machinery. Between the parameter of your palms this beach could be any flat, beige slant, sloping incrementally downhill until it meets the water's spume. If you don't look around for contrary evidence, you might find yourself, indeed, at the Dunes.

Then later, when you grow up, come back for a look, only then drop your palms and take in the full panorama.

You'll be surprised by how much that old trick-of-the-palms hid. A string of mills, Gary Works and more, run for a mile or so to your left, and to your right, NIPSCO, the power plant with the curvaceous cooling stack that looks like, but is not, a nuke. All the stacks are gray from this distance, like photographs enlarged past their range of focus, or as if nestled behind a sheer gray curtain, freestanding shadows. The steel mills in particular appear as if materialized out of the grain of distance and memory, specks that gather to form first a silhouette, then a solid body. This seeing and not seeing, the awareness cloaked in the refusal to see, is the reason why, no matter where I am—in a water taxi in Baltimore, say, or peering through a spotty train window while trundling through rural Poland—when I encounter, suddenly, the hulk of a factory or mill wall, looming shadowy and rusted, glinting, always, like the violet of twilight, even in the middle of the day, I feel the gloom of déjà vu, the experience of memory where there is no memory, a return of a phantom moment of place and space that I did not allow myself to notice when it was really there.

THE APOCALYPSE, DARLING

Interior Landscapes 1959–

I don't remember where I heard the unconscious described as sensual affinities we are unaware of, yet think about constantly, an endless newsreel projected onto the inside of the forehead that we feel behind the hairline but can't see. This is how it is with me and my Old Country wasteland, the reason I am a pessimist, expecting the worst so assiduously it seems I also almost wish for brokenness, the reason when I see the desolate Calumet Region of my childhood spread out like a centerfold through the rental car windshield I feel not as if I am returning, but rather that I am awakening, opening my eyes to the familiar wound—that scraped gray earth, that slag and smoke and muddy gravel, even the unlikely hope of a bright blue painted wall that by its brightness brings attention to the bleak—continuing as it always has even while I am away, dreaming the earth is also, sometimes, still, naturally green.

THE BEE-U-TEE-FULL
OLD COUNTRY

Indiana 2008

By *green* I don't mean the golf course, so unnaturally green, the surface of beauty with no body beneath.

Once beyond the gate, in search of the wedding, Linnea drives us down and around the winding lane of driveways and cul-de-sacs, past clean picture windows and open garages, arriving at one of the smaller split-level glass and brick ranches surrounding the golf course. As we enter through the open garage, the first thing we notice, above the SUVs and golf carts, are the angels of this plasticized heaven, by which I mean a row of plastic female torsos, trunks of women's bodies, neck to waist, with old-timey lingerie shop swell and narrow.

The torso collection hangs like guardians from the walls above the golf cart and the craft supply shelving—department store mannequin trunks propped up with steel hooks the way most people who live in ranch houses store skis or soccer equipment or fishing poles in their garages. None of us has met anyone but the bride and groom at this party, and none of us wants to cross the threshold of the bride's sister's home alone, so Linnea, her siblings, and their spouses gather here, chuckling and scattering and adjusting our hems, waiting for Linnea's brother and brother-in-law to change from car shorts to dress suits beneath a chorus of headless, nipple-less cleavage, as if this were the waiting room of Willy Wonka's Maidenform Factory.

I turn to Linnea's youngest sister, not the doctor, but the one who used to pose for the tags on department store swimsuits, the pretty pinup girl sibling who has transformed her gifts as an advertising model into a more long-standing, bankable talent for writing marketing copy. *What do you think they do with all these bods?* I ask her. She is herself shaped more like the mannequins than any of the rest of us, but she's a creative professional with college ambitions for her nearly grown daughters, years beyond making a living from showing off her torso. She shrugs and laughs. Everything about her father's quick-fire wedding is a curiosity.

I become then too conscious of all our torsos. Linnea's sisters are wearing summer muslin, the redheaded surgeon in relatively modest spaghetti straps but her ex-model sister's neckline plunging to her upper waist. Linnea's brother's wife and I both wear bosomy sundresses, while the men are all wearing dress shirts and ties. The demarcation between the men and the women is mostly clear: the men are buttoned-up-and-knotted, the women wearing patterned fabric against bare skin. But then there is Linnea, not so much straddling as betraying biology in her off-white linen men's suit, her powder blue dress shirt unbuttoned at the collar, the Italian-stallion charm, a golden horn, hanging on a gold chain around her neck.

The constellation of D-cup torsos hovering above our heads is the first sign that we have reentered the Old Country we once knew well but have nearly forgotten, the dead old land Linnea and I had long ago reinvented ourselves out of — a country where the defining lines between women's and men's bodies were not ironic, but inviolate, where women swelled and bent, where men squared off and stood over, away from the women, no drag show this, but a land where the people play their roles in earnest.

If the torsos hanging over us had kept their heads, they would have shaken out their torrents of Miss America hair, exposed the long lines of their beautiful Old Country necks. They would have tossed back their heads and laughed.

WOMEN'S WORK

North Suburban Chicago 1988

The first night I met the former swimsuit model, Linnea's young-est sister, she was whipping through the dusting, wiping down the windows, scrubbing down all the counter surfaces, dressed in a clingy T-shirt and gym shorts, revealing enough to allow me to see how similar her body was to Linnea's, so curious that the same attributes—long firm thighs and trim hips—could be bath-ing-suit-tag girly on one sister, cowboy handsome in another.

And judging by the speed with which she cleaned the house, clearly, like Linnea, her sister knew how to work. Linnea had learned how to get things done working the women's hosiery department at Kmart, while her sisters did the same at the local Mr. Steak, all of them out of the house, earning money for college early. The Michigan Swede wasn't going to help them out, even though he had the dough, and who wouldn't rather, in the days before the divorce, be out working instead of home, dealing with Dad's drinking, dealing with Mom's suspicions that her husband was selling more than insurance to the neighbor ladies.

Linnea's youngest sister was still single when I met her, just done with college and living in a tiny suburban apartment with her newly divorced Mom. Linnea and I were twenty-something, big-hair-and-leather-clad lesbians then, driving down from Minneapolis for the holidays. This was the 1980s when queers were sort of out-and-proud, but not like we are now: gay weddings were comparatively rare then, the only queers on TV the likes of Elton John and Boy George, obvious homos but not saying so yet. Linnea and I stood out against the tableau of her mother and sisters.

Linnea's youngest sister wore her hair long then, strawberry blond with white blond streaks. I told Linnea her sis looked just like Ann-Margret in *Bye-Bye Birdie*—curvy, smiling with her eyes while her lips pouted, the same square cut of chin that made Linnea look good in a businessman's fedora, but gave her sister's face a star-of-stage-and-screen profile. Since then, when we talk about her to our friends we call her the Ann-Margret-sister. Not that the surgeon sister wasn't girly too, the skinniest of the three, her long red hair strewn around her head on whatever couch she found to fall asleep on in those years she was completing her round-the-clock residency training. She amazed me by waking up in a streak and reapplying her eyeliner with one hand. I have no sisters, so the habits of Linnea's fascinated me.

I noticed, for instance, that Mom and the Ann-Margret-sister kept their nail polish in the refrigerator—a small thing but the sort of domestic detail that was a news flash to me. My own mother never used nail polish or eyeliner or perfume, perhaps because gym teachers don't get dressed up for work, perhaps because no one taught her. Linnea's mom was an East Coast Italian American, Linnea's dad the Michigan Swede who dragged her away from her family to the Midwest. It wasn't until I met Linnea's Jersey aunts and cousins that I saw the fundamental source of her Mom's salon hair color, her mani-pedis, her Italian shoes and quality brassieres, all of which even influenced Linnea, albeit in a more oblique fashion, back in the day when she performed Patsy Cline drag in the downtown Minneapolis bars. The Italian American Feminine is as much a tradition in Linnea's family as her grandmother's recipe for pork sauce.

SWEDISH ITALIAN

New Jersey/Michigan/Illinois 1960s

And note that the Italian American Feminine is an impatient feminine. A work-ethic feminine. A talk-with-her-hands, shout-out-to-the-saints, cut-anyone-who-crossed-her-family feminine.

Linnea's mother set the first standard, when her kids were young, dancing in the kitchen in her stocking feet to songs on the a.m. radio, ignoring all thoughts of him and what he'd say later when he came home to dishes still not done and a kitchen full of laughing. Too loose for his standards.

These were the standards of a hard-drinking Michigan Swede who punished his children if the finger he ran across the top of the fridge came back dusty, standards that may have instilled in them their propensity for hard, fast, and focused work, the work that helped them propel themselves so far beyond the reach of this father.

DON'T ASK DON'T TELL

Interstate 1980–2008

Picture him, white hair, pale skin, a tall blocky torso and long knobby legs, towing his trailer along the Interstate during snowbird migration season. He's the one with an American flag decal on his cap and a T-shirt that reads SWEDISH AMERICAN and PROUD. He's the one with the Bush-Quayle bumper sticker on the back of his sedan and an American flag decal on the back window of his trailer. He's the one leaning over the dimly lit American Legion bar with its 1970 leather-upholstered walls, his pale, unsmiling face echoed in the mottled glass of the old mirror behind the bottles, muttering about Communists and Democrats and public schools that suck all the good American money.

He'd mutter about the queers too, but he doesn't like to admit they exist, and anyway he blames the queers on the Communists, so he's covered.

I can see him, but I can't see inside the way he sees his children. When he visits his son he complains about what's playing on TV. When he visits his grandchildren he complains about the ways his daughters raise their kids. When he visits Linnea he avoids the obvious—her men's clothes, her female spouse, her lefty politico lawn signs—and asks her for things anyone would know she doesn't have. Such as, could she get him tickets to the Republican National Convention?

He is aiming his trailer toward some kind of dunes, and like any of us he doesn't always see how the terrain around him withers.

THE CHILDREN'S CRIMES, ACCORDING TO THE FATHER, AS IMAGINED BY THE DAUGHTER-IN-LAW HE DOES NOT ACKNOWLEDGE

Minneapolis 2008

His youngest daughter must be having the change of life.

If his son pulled himself up, shaved, hid those tattoos, he'd make a man's kind of money.

Look at his middle daughter, who's done so well. He taught her the value of money.

His oldest is fine except for that problem, but she holds a good job so her employers must be tolerant.

His first wife was an exciting woman before she got so angry. Those Italians. Or maybe her family in Jersey—they never liked the Swedes— were the ones who poisoned her against him?

Women love a strong, organized man with a good income.

He's not drinking lately. It bothers his stomach. Did we see he's taken off a few pounds?

His new special lady doesn't think that woman who lives with his oldest girl looks like she could be one of those. She must not have met a strong man with a good income.

He doesn't understand why his children aren't warm like their mother. Sometimes, ha-ha, she was too hot.

His hand lifts, as if to reach, but he sets it back down again. This is the violet hour; the engine of his humanness is waiting, this wedding that might have been his first but is instead his last, the green ahead.

WHAT'S PRESENT IN TIME FUTURE II

Chicago 2015

The future barely contained in this time past is the rogue daughter-in-law surprised to find she does come into the father's view, a new present tense in the body politic, during which time not all, but some, of the fathers—the governors, mayors, judges, and presidents—might say not her name, but the name of her kind, not a new world, but a few sweet hollows of respite, better times before worsening times, clearings that require her own adjustment of view.

But not yet.

THE VIOLET HOUR

Indiana 2008

Meanwhile, inside the golf course wedding house, a maelstrom of strangers gather—strangers to us, just as from their point of view a smaller vortex of strangers gathers in the garage, one long-familiar family encroaching on another.

All family constellations change, and with each marriage comes another link in the extended family solar system, but it's more comfortable, more expected, when that link comes from under rather than over, from the grandchildren not the grand-mother. And that this wedding is happening in the home of the bride's sister and brother-in-law means that we invade the citadel of another family's grandmother, and in this matriarch's realm we will be outnumbered by at least five-to-one.

Knowing this, we hover, our generation huddling in sun-dresses, spaghetti straps and ties, under the torso angels who, without meaning to, convey our position in the body-middle years, all of us here with the lovers we've chosen, all of us in or close to our 40s and aware, if we lower our palms, that youth sulks far down one side of the beach, old age beckons from the other, and inside this house our father, or our spouse's father, is about to re-marry and change everything.

On the other side of the door another family huddles, and through the glass the unnatural green of the golf course slopes and gathers. Before we cross over I pause to imagine that other family there, long-stemmed cocktail glasses in hand, staring out into the green as the future rushes into the vacuum. Which future? The wasteland forcing its way in through the gates, the turf and sod peeling back to reveal what must be the same chemical-leached ground as the rest of the region, the apocalypse, Darling, encroaching slowly, unfurling as if in a time-lapsed film?

Or will this be bloom from a corpse, the gray gradually regenerating green? Is that the Holy Supper plate on the dining room wall, spinning over the family table of these soon-to-be new in-laws, this attorney who will marry these new-old lovers, the attorney's wife who will smile hard from the sidelines even as her husband entertains the crowd from what he will call his chapel on the green, take this man, take this wife, take my wife, please?

A shimmer of light refracts from the television set over the bar, bright with another holy or unholy alliance, the Crosstown Series, Sox versus Cubs, broadcasting back from the direction we came, White Sox U.S. Cellular Field, just over the East Side centerfold, where the Indiana Skyway dumps traffic bound for the South Side of Chicago. The reflection from the opening pitch illuminates the bright airborne ball, an accidental gyre of afternoon light, as somebody's family lines up along the glass in print dresses and heels and summer sports coats, sparkly glasses raised in a toast as another family opens the door from the garage into the kitchen, ready to cross this pre-wedding Purgatory, as the ground seems to shudder and one future, or another, approaches.

PART III

NOTHING

WITH

NOTHING

THE WE WHO

Indiana 2008

We cross the wedding threshold, meet the receiving line of smiling strangers, two families who, according to the linguistics of weddings, are soon to be ceremoniously joined.

But though the bride and groom know each other from fifty years back, their families have developed in each other's absence, and so nobody peering across the divide is quite sure who is who. Is this frowning woman stacking plates and utensils in the kitchen a daughter or the caterer? The winky fellow behind the bar is whose brother? Whose cousin? And the frizzy blond in the madras blouse and sandals too casual for even a golf course wedding, is she a cousin too, or just a family friend?

Everyone introduces themselves but nobody keeps anyone clear. Though we couldn't look less related, one of them (who was she?) asks three of us—the Swedish Italian ex-model, the petite Greek ex-rock-band groupie, the bleached and tattooed ex-alkie lesbian—*are you the sisters?*

Sisters-in-law, one of us crows, no point in explaining who is legally or un-legally married to whom, we who have known each other for so many years but have never before been daughters of a common groom.

Our Lady of the Intercom, the bride's sister, greets us wearing a neat white pantsuit, her hair lacquered into a gray-blond pageboy, her eyes blinky behind the thick lenses of her heavy-framed glasses. She looks more like a Manhattan lady editor than a golf course matron, and she is pricklier than her sister, not pink, her voice gravely, ice cubes in her cocktail chiming as she looks us over without asking names. Linnea in her gentleman's summer linen suit, one hand grasping her brother's elbow, reaches out to shake her hand.

Well hello. Linnea enunciates, as the lady leans closer. *You must be the lady,* she says, *of the house.* Linnea possesses the social charm to pull off phrases like lady-of-the-house without sounding foolish.

The lady blinks at Linnea's cropped gray hair—the same cut as usual, nearly a crew cut. She had it trimmed by her favorite barber before we left Minneapolis. The lady blinks as Linnea continues. *I'm the groom's daughter.* She is practically shouting at the blinking lady, who clutches her cocktail, who blinks and stares again at Linnea's bristled hairline.

Then Linnea gestures up toward the tall redheaded man beside her. *And this,* Linnea says, *is my BABY brother.*

The lady's smile is wide and static. We know this one. We've seen this before, though not so much lately as we did in the old days. She must not understand why this smiling man has introduced himself as a daughter. She has that look of one hypnotized by thunder. Linnea's arm is outstretched. The lady speaks without parting her teeth.

I don't know, says the lady, *what we're talking about here.*

UNREAL CITY

Minneapolis 1987–Yesterday

What we are talking about here is our daily reentry into, and departure from, wastelands we thought we'd long left behind, diplomatic discord Linnea tells me she no longer sees.

I see. In elevators, in certain restaurants, at workplace functions, leaving her Jersey cousin's wedding as we waited for the valet, where we, the two of us, had not been seen before, were unknown, unreal. Usually this is, and has been, the gaze of conspicuously heterosexual men, the men who look at women in that way that some men (and to be honest, the occasional woman) look at women. That commercial exchange in which no money changes hands. The substance is the body, the woman's body. The profit is pleasure, the looker's pleasure. The man (or the woman) being the type whose looking is more than collection, more than intake, looking as ransacking, as a wasting, plundering verb.

When we were a bit younger this happened more than it does now. Let's say Linnea and I were in what was then one of our favorite restaurants in downtown Minneapolis, with the scratched wooden booths and the orange art deco lights behind the bar, where the valets and bartenders knew Linnea's name because she used to tend bar there herself. The customers were not our usual gang of motley-and-many-gendered girly boys and boy-girls, but instead were middle-aged straight guys, out with their colleagues or wives. Some of these guys—in this place it was usually guys—first saw me, then looked at me, into me, woman, breasts and boots, blond and baby-less. Older, but perhaps, their looks said, not yet too old. Assuming themselves the arbiters of not just my ass but my age. Then looked at my companion, the man in a business suit who was suddenly, no, not a man, yes, no, her body, my husband's body, throbbing between, as she looped her elbow into mine, my escort yes, and this guy was still looking, but his look ricocheted from longing to incineration—and now this was, and is, always a man, because women who look at women already know how to see trans-masculine people who live in the country of women. I'd know that look anywhere, carnal confusion, colonial implosion. Linnea and my burgeoning city was his burning city, his wasteland our garden, pleasure interrupted by *Darling, what* are *we talking about here?*

LILACS OUT OF A DEAD LAND

Indiana 2008

Whose wasteland is whose garden; whose garden is whose wasteland?

What we're talking about here is golf courses and antique-lit downtown chophouses, with doors flung open, queers who remake themselves a home in transparent cities remade atop older cities that are not gone, blue-skinned steel mills still pumping along the bared lakeshore, prairie grass and sand-strewn beaches between, water throwing itself against the dunes, the insistence of life, continuing, polluted, persisting, the noon fog of homelands colliding. Their corpse our bloom. Our blooming their scorched earth. The seeds of what we feared as teenagers fleeing have become the lilacs of our return. Our old and new cities, real, unreal, our bodies, unreal, real, flow past, pass though one another, and in the crease, the juncture between?

Linnea holds out her hand to the lady of the house, the beleaguered wife here on the green who has been, I might as well say it, already, for hours, or days or months, and is now, still, drinking. I was once a drinker; I always see the drinkers. The drinkers see me too, especially men who drink, or used to drink, especially the ones who used to drink but stopped drinking through willpower instead of some god. Those guys like something about me, but what? The patina of misspent surrender, perhaps. The whiff of familiar burning.

I have not forgotten what it's like to be wanted while wasted, by the wasted, nor have I forgotten all the ways to be wasted is to be used up carelessly, be a weak and emaciated territory, an engine worn down to the bolts. The lady is wasted and so can't quite see us, or sees some other us that we don't see, we who have invaded her home on a Saturday afternoon in June to watch these old folks, her generation, remaking themselves into their memory of the teenagers they used to be. Linnea's tall brother is laughing. Linnea is grinning. I am watching, looking, taking away, for my own pleasure, not carnality but meaning, evidence of lilacs I long ago left behind, signs that the wasteland might be, might not be, might finally be, re-greening, or will never re-green.

But this is not even my side of the family so perhaps I have no right. Is this our old country reckoning, Darling, or just another family wedding?

LAQUEARIA

Indiana 2008

Then we cross into the house of glass. The walls are mostly windows looking out on the unreal greenery, clipped shrubbery and the statuary—bared torsos of goddesses, their white robes falling from their hips, their shoulders and chests bared. These truncated angels don't watch over from above, like the others, but twist, their bare nipples facing us, their necks stretched away, turned toward the swells and hollows of the course, as if watching for intruders posing as golfers.

The walls inside, panels of plaster between stretches of glass, feature lithographs of more upper bodies, women again, more goddesses emerging from fallen drapery or perhaps art school models, striking the usual pose, the folds of the fallen sheets echoing curves of breast or shoulder.

I point out these galleries to Linnea, outside, then inside. What is it with all these bods? We look at each other and shrug. Perhaps these people collect torsos the way others do Star Trek figurines or model trains or Mardi Gras masks. Is there some unspoken breast story in this family, as there is in most families? Breast enhancement? Breast reduction? Breast cancer? The attraction might be the eternal youth of upright breasts, or maybe the charms of a colonial gaze, ownership of the classic curve and turn of women's upper body exhibited the way some might display landscapes of the Old World, inherited memory located in the simplicity of nostalgia. And now here is Linnea standing in front of these emblems, the classical feminine, the anti-feminine. She doesn't like to call attention to the fact that she has breasts, but under the comfortable lines of her suit her own torso is not so much hidden as not evident. The men of this stranger's family shake her hand, wink at me, let their gaze graze my cleavage always asking me, not Linnea, if I am the groom's daughter, not letting on whether they, too, have no idea of what we're talking about here.

The torsos twist and sway as if alone in their dressing room, vain angels, inattentive guardians, as TV screens suspended overhead feature the twist of a White Sox pitcher's frame. The pitcher delivers another strike, and the crowd in the background undulates, the lit inner dome of some kind of chapel, this fleshy laquearia. The Cubs' batter's torso turns. He swings; he misses for the third time, lets the bat drop from his fingers. The crowd twitters and scatters. Bare-breasted bods glimmer in this glassy light. White-shirted men toss, connect, dash toward the win. This is the chapel of the land that made us, a land we left in search of another body, where there are breasts but also baseball, where there is baseball but also breasts.

O CITY, CITY

Minneapolis 2007

The city Linnea and I have not yet left is the city where we sat with our friends around a table covered in patterned white cloth, tattered in parts. From a distance, if you did not know what we were talking about here, you might think we were women and men, but we who have gathered understand this communion of male-and-female women. We sat before a holy bowl of nuts and fruit, Clementines, pears, persimmon, and pomegranate. One of us knew the way to open the pomegranate, pealing the skin, inserting a thumb, separating the orb, a world asunder, seeds bursting, sweet cascade. The crack of a pecan and walnut shell. The dusky flesh of persimmon and sharp burst of pomegranate seed. Sweet and salt, fingers to tongue. We toasted, some with scotch, some with juice. To chosen family. We bared our bods by telling stories. The roommate we'd let (we didn't know we loved her then) rub oil into our nipples in the hopes our breasts would grow. That drag king we didn't love but fucked in bar bathrooms for just one week before the need subsided. The gorgeous stranger who offered herself to us in an airport waiting room, whom we considered but (regretfully) turned down. The toy we preferred, the long one, or the thick one, the admission we made that we liked it inside and long, or not long but thick, or not inside but outside, long or thick, inside her but not us, or inside both of us. We were not sitting in the city that made us, each of us having made ourselves over in other cities. The lands of wreck and memory that made us carried on without full knowledge of the city we had made in the wake of all we'd left behind. Fingers to tongue, fruit to language. The pomegranate burst, a fountain, an invention, that fragment of grace we'd made way here to taste.

BURNINGBURNING

Illinois or Indiana Mill Country, 20th or 21st Century

As the groom means to be remade in this glass room overlooking the green, against hills, the swells of golfers, the shushing of sprinklers, the hum of fat-wheeled carts, the pump of the mills. No, no the mills are not visible through this glass, but listen, can you hear them, not far from here, just beyond the stage sets?

These mills are the reason that Southern and Eastern Europeans, Mexicans, and African American descendants of slaves from the South first migrated to this stretch of Lake Michigan shore between Northeast Illinois and Northwest Indiana. The golf course is only a painted scrim. If we dropped the curtain we'd see the tracks, the silos, the gray mill roofs, the smokestacks, the sound of the beach, along the Dunes

washingnnn washinnnnn washingnnn

the crack of waves if the day is windy, where there is water, where there is sand, where there is the constant spew and light from the stacks, flinging flames, burning.

Between the stacks is the sand where as a teenager I walked these Dunes, a rubbish of dead fish littering the wake of the waves. But I will see for myself, thirty years later, just after the close of this wedding, that now the beach is clean. A park ranger will explain how it started in the 1980s, soon after I left: the cleanup, the environmental rescue, the turn. Where there were my dunes, now there are better dunes. A lively ecosystem, the park brochures say. A variegated habitat the brochure will read, to which I will now amend: a habitat that speaks to the erotic charge of life. The old dunes that were dying are now living. Where there was scorched ground, here now land has scarred over and new growth is ready for its close-up.

How much of the ruins his children knew remains, how much is rebuilt, how much still burning?

THE TATTOO MERCHANT

Inside an Inaccurate
Indiana Fantasy 2008

And so we gather in this golf course living room, on folding chairs set up where a sofa usually sits. Linnea and I accidentally sit on the bride's side instead of the groom's, and her redheaded surgeon sister joins us, along with kids and husband, and we are all settled there, me on the end, my shoulder grazing the rough brick of the fireplace, before we notice our seating mistake. By then we don't want to take the trouble to move, especially since the groom's family is far too few to claim one whole side of the room.

And there I sit when some old uncle, yellow-shirted, keys and coins jangling in his pocket, squeezes up along the fireplace wall, making passage where there is no passage, a camera hanging around his neck, ostensibly pushing up to the front to get a better snapshot. He straddles chairs, clatters forward, and it makes no sense that he wouldn't just walk up the center aisle, until he gets to me. Standing behind, bending over, he places his palms on each bare shoulder and squeezes, leaning into my neck, whispering into my ear, his vanity requiring, but receiving, no response. *Nice tattoo*, he growls, and he squeezes me again.

Linnea sits just two inches away, turns and glares at this bumpy old uncle, as any husband would. Only then does this guy take his hands off my shoulders. Only then am I sure he does not know what we are talking about here.

He punches Linnea on the shoulder, ha-ha, guy-to-guy. In the linguistics of the Old Country I am a blond with visible boobs and tattoos, a good-time gal hanging in this gallery of broken torsos, still smelling of the wind of some familiar burning, his nothing touching nothing of me, my real body, Linnea's body, not to them what our bodies are to us, made of fragments of a language still, here, unheard.

THE GOLF COURSE NUPTIALS, AS IMPRECISELY RECALLED WITH UNDISGUISED BIAS, AND WITHOUT APPROVAL FROM HER SPOUSE, BY THE DAUGHTER-IN-LAW THE GROOM HAS NOT YET ACKNOWLEDGED

Indiana 2008

And so the pink lady stands before her brother-in-law, the divorce attorney who will (re)marry her, cleavage heaving prettily in her low-cut, off-white bridal gown, the torso angels all around her breathing in tandem, her face starry with what even she will say later was the unexamined high of marrying this man she'd only (re)met a few months before, the man she'd loved before he was a man, before she was a woman, more than a half-century ago, in adolescence that was then living but was now certainly dead, or had been dead and which she was now (re)living, or willing back to life. And her husband-to-be stands by her side, besotted and silent, the cat who caught the canary, as they say, as I say in retrospect, not because the description is original but because this is one of those moments where I think oh, this is why they say *he looks like the cat who caught the canary*, because indeed he does look just like that cat, and his bride, in that bosom-baring gown, is sure as hell some kinda canary.

All of which the divorce attorney, a square, thick, bald guy in designer eyewear who looks more like an old-time Hollywood agent than a steel-town lawyer, does not say, but might have said, because that's the way he talks, like one of the cheerful thugs from the musical *Guys and Dolls*, about to roll the dice and break out into some kinda Sinatra ballad.

A kind of cadence, to be fair, I understand, 'cause I'm from around here too, 'cause I got uncles back dere in Chicago dat talk a helluva lot like dis.

So welcome to da Chapel on the Green, he says.

As ya know, dese guys scheduled their wedding on a day when da Cubs are playing da Sox. So ha-ha we're gonna make dis short, he says.

(His eyes drift up to the TV screen, the game, another slow pitch he's missing.)

So welcome ta my home, made possible, ya know, by my successful practice as a divorce attorney, ha-ha, he says.

(*The house divorce built*, the ex-model's husband whispers.)

And to the groom I offer dis warning. Once you marry wona dese sisters there's no way outa dis deal, he says.

(Our Lady of the Intercom smiles harder and chimes the ice in her drink.)

So welcome to da family, he says to our canary-swallowing groom.

(Linnea elbows me and surreptitiously points. As the bride's granddaughter recites the wedding poem, chosen to celebrate this lost-and-found love story, the lyrics of that Nat King Cole song, "Unforgettable," beyond the glass, behind the bride and groom, in the direction the torso statues turn to watch, a tawny dog, without a leash, is taking a dump on the green.)

So with dis ring I pronounce you married, so go ahead and kiss your bride, he says.

(And the groom does kiss the bride, a helluva kiss, the smooch of an impatient high school boy who finally gets his date alone between the lockers, during which time the groom's daughters look away. Later the redheaded surgeon says to me, *I wonder why*

Dad didn't kiss the bride, and I realize, though she was right there, next to me, the whole time, some power had plucked her from what she did not want to see, her father as the teenage boy he can no longer be, her father alive in a life that lived and burned away long before her family came to be, and already she has refused to (re)member, and I think again, how lucky for the old Swede, that all his kids showed up for this wedding.)

PART IV

WHAT THE

WATER

SAID

SHANTIH

Indiana 2009

Later I will drive back again, once more to the wasteland, with questions. It will be February and it will be snowing, and the waves will not even whisper their familiar *washingnnn wash-innnnn*. The waves will be frozen, caught in mid-arc, an ice shelf the park brochures call it, but I will see less a shelf than an expanse, an existence, fragments of a glacier, the ice plain. The sound will be that of a white wind, an ice wind, and the noiseless February snow.

I will see the steel mills, still burning. And the land around the mills still wasted by mercury, lead, cyanide, ammonia, arsenic, benzene, fluoride, nitrates, oil, grease, and yes, still slagged and seared, the view from the Indiana Skyway still gray rubble, interrupted by the grace of Gary Works blue, but now I will add that Gary Works is still the largest working steel-making facility in the Western Hemisphere, and I will add the jobs, the girders, the skyscraper cores, the donated steel holding up St. Michael's the Archangel Catholic Church in my mother's old neighborhood on the South Side of Chicago, the fifty-foot-tall steel Picasso sculpture, fabricated in Gary and moved to Daley Plaza where it shadows downtown office workers (I was one once) scuttling to and from their desks, the lives that have been created — my life in fact — by migrations drawn to the magnet of big steel.

The nature of what humans make, what humans change.

Take the Dunes themselves. The ranger I meet will have plenty of time to talk to me, because it is February, it's snowing, there is hardly anyone on the lakefront when I trek out through the flurries, toward the ice shelf, the beach pavilion empty, shuttered up, only the wind visiting at this time of year. A couple — a man and a woman — will be leaving the beach as I arrive, their faces obscured by scarves. *Brisk,* I will call out to them as we pass, and the man will laugh and say *ya think?* He will be too young to remember this beach the way I do, but at least we will share this desolate grace, the water a body frozen in motion, in a moment of upheaval, breath held, the chest full, a cold and unlivable plain, but not a waste. The ice shelf will melt and where there is ice there will be water, and then, *washingnnn,* the water song will return.

I am also older than the ranger at the interpretive center. When I tell him I used to come to this beach, cutting school in the 1970s, I'll imagine him thinking *before I was born.* Still, he will know the story. When I say I remember it was ugly then, polluted, stinking with dead fish, he will say *yes,* and speak of cleanup and science and preservation. He will tell me how little by little the park service reclaims the toxic dumps, re-greens them, re-invents them as parks. He will show me a printout from Google maps, a road that winds around one of the working mills to new greenery built over a dump, opening this coming summer, he'll puff, as if he'd built the new park himself.

I will watch the free film, about bogs and rookeries and watersheds and tall dunes the lake wind keeps pushing inland. Dunes shadow mill fields or mill fields shadow dunes. Here there is steel and no sand, and there is sand but no steel, then steel and sand and steel again. Yet the park service films leave out the mills, and later, driving by the mills, I will find the beach becomes immediately hard to remember. When the ranger tells me of the park built over the landfill I will be with him, yes, such a relief, such hope, this re-greening, but later I will try to find the new park, following his map; on every likely road winding around every one of the mills the signs will say unauthorized vehicles are not allowed, and men in hard hats will step out of security huts and peer at me pulled over in my rental car, fingering maps, staring up at the stacks, as I wonder if the mill toxins can really be partitioned off into park and not-park, wondering whether there really is a line between the smoke and the sand.

I won't want to try to explain what I am looking for to anyone wearing a security badge—because what would I say? I want to see if change is possible, if wastelands can revive, if lost love and re-found love can coexist, if unloving fathers can become loving, even lovable? Do we live in the Old Country or the new?

February. The wind brisk and the sun setting and the signs telling me to scram—little chance that some guy with a badge will want to help the blond in the rental car find a hidden beach. So I will turn around, head back to the Skyway, leave Indiana, drive the fifteen miles back to the warm hotel room in Chicago where the first steel I see out the window is the Sears Tower.

But before I try to find the new park and fail, give up, hightail it out of there, I will drive the other way, deeper into Indiana where I'll find another kind of surprise. Along the shore, in a residential district interrupted by national lakeshore beaches and train stations for the South Shore Line running back and forth from downtown Chicago, a stretch of half-renovated architectural wonders, the biggest a hybrid octagon, the House of Tomorrow, with faceted porches and a steel-framed experimental design. I'll stop to read the historical markers. These are the Century of Progress homes, renovation underway, leftovers from the 1933–34 World's Fair, hybrid homesteads, experiments in living that some developer, hoping to turn the Indiana lakeshore into a vacationland for wealthy Chicagoans, carted over from the city by barge.

The vacationland never took off, but the homes are still there, new bodies from the dead. I'll be riveted, staring out my windshield, buzzing with the ingenuity and erotics of hybrid form, the grace of human making, god alive in the ruins, until snow begins to obscure my windshield, and I turn on the wipers and move on.

Later I'll read that the original version of the House of Tomorrow had glass walls that became too hot in the summer, causing the air conditioning to fail, so the revised house on the Indiana shore has windows that open, inviting circulation, making allowances for wind, human nature recast in a movable glass and octagon frame.

Shantih shantih shantih. Peace that surpasses understanding.

Some mild peace may be all I seek, between the Skyway and the Dunes, some fragment of evidence, what human nature still tries to build, fails to build, tries, a hope not for April, but for May, lilacs bursting into plump bouquets, new growth a smell, not sweet, not salt, not water, not steel, not scrap. Not just scrap. What was the old is now old-and-new.

PART V

FRAGMENTS

AGAINST

RUINS

POST-NUPTIAL

Indiana Golf Course 2008

After wedding vows, set against plate glass, lit up by putting-green eleganza, outlined by baseball's low drone and attentive breasts of headless angels.

After the Swedish appetizer buffet and after the toasts the bride's daughter had practiced, but the groom's son—no wedding rules expert, marrying his own bride in Vegas—doesn't know he is supposed to prepare.

After the catered salmon and wild rice and after the dissolution back into familiar family folds—too hard to keep trying to find ways into these strangers' conversations when we may never meet again.

After the ritual of the bride and groom's first dance, becoming inverse ritual when they break away—not the bride with her father, the groom with his mother, as they would have danced if they were they still young and their own parents still living—this bride reaching for her son, this groom for his daughters, or some of his daughters.

After all this, I sit upon the shoreline, a folding chair at the edge, still believing I will get away with simple observation, enjoying the benefits of the unacknowledged. Not my family to set in order.

And I so watch, as if this were any wedding. All weddings are send-offs into marriage, never the marriage itself, and this one is no different. It will be a month or so before we hear news of the usual fissures—first fights, first refusals, the collision of 150 combined years of preference and habit, two stubborn old Upper Michigan Swedes who marry their common nostalgia and each find themselves with a new body in their bed, this constant corporeal presence that now they have to get to know.

If falling in love is an arrangement with hope, living with love is something again, breaking hope down into individual beads, a daily kneading of stone, finding water in the sound of water that emerges out of the rattle of where there seems to be no water. Like god, like home, like the names we call ourselves, love is not just what we find or remember but also what we make. This is no different for old sweethearts, or for new.

But in this violet hour, the wedding day subsiding, I watch the pretty bride, still so much in the pink, a rare newlywed wife, enjoying her own wedding. Her skin is so smooth, impossibly smooth for age seventy-five, whether by Botox or good skin products or happiness, I can't know, but she looks as if this wedding joy has made her smoother, her eyes focused so very far back, sixty years, to her high school formal perhaps, inhabiting the young woman she was then, a girl none of us will ever meet.

And I watch my father-in-law dance with his daughters. The redheaded surgeon is polite, professional; the ex-model is still stiff with complaints, resistant, rebuffing, telling him as if he were meeting her for the first time what the rest of us already knew, that she does not, no, will not, no, cannot dance, not with him or at all, she is simply not someone who dances, but he persists, long enough that she does finally, rigid in his embrace, turn a few embarrassed box steps.

His youngest daughter breaks away, the music still playing— the song still Nat King Cole's "Unforgettable," their song, though I keep mistaking it for "Strangers in the Night." I look around for Linnea, wondering if her father will ask her to dance next, wondering how that will come off, here at this wedding where half the guests think Linnea is a man. While there must be some wedding someplace where grooms dance with their sons, I doubt it happens too often in Northwest Indiana. But just as I spot Linnea, hovering back in a corner, hiding—she does not want to, no, will not dance with her father—I feel the man's fingers squeezing my wrists. *You're next,* my father-law whispers to me. *If you want.*

I don't want. No. But worse, I didn't know he could see me there, watching from the edge. All these years of not being seen, and now I don't wish him to see me. That he does see me is no comfort, is a crack opening under our feet. I do not, no, will not, no, cannot dance, am not someone who dances with anyone but Linnea. But not just that. After years of ghosting corners, watching but unwatched, to be suddenly seen—embraced too quickly, too tightly around the wrist—feels like runaway greening, a crack under long-established footing, the crazy, swallowing growth before it all implodes.

No thank you, I tell him. I will stay here in the margins. I will not step over.

No thank you, the torso chorus titters and repeats.

POST–APOCALYPSE, THE RAIN

Indiana 2008

Then when the rain begins it is an uncanny rain. The party is breaking down, the ballgame over, the televisions dark, the caterers clearing the dishes, guests hovering, wondering whether or not to wait for the storm to pass through.

Linnea and I stand with the Divorce Attorney in the glass doorway of his veranda, the same doorway where earlier his wife had stood with her cocktail, waving away the waiter offering her the salmon plate. *Not now, I'm drinking,* she said, saluting him with her glass. This is the port of salutation, a deck overlooking a minimized world, a changing or unchanging plain of shivering shrubbery, of stone torsos turning on the spine of a tightening sky as we feel the wind pick up, interrupting the usual flow of a Midwestern summer shower.

Look, the attorney says, smoking a cigar with one hand, waving out at the soggy greenery with the other. *Everythin's turned around here today. It's even rainin sideways.*

We don't know if he means the late-life wedding, the cross-league ballgame, the groom's daughter in a man's suit, or just the sudden bad weather, but it is indeed raining sideways, the downpour running not down but parallel to the ground.

But when the rain stops, all at once, no tapering, over the green we see two arcs of light. *And now lookat dat,* the attorney says. *Can ya believe? Now a double rainbow?*

The bride walks by just then and I nudge her shoulder. *Look,* I say. *Did you see the rainbows?* She peers out. *Ohhh.* She gasps. *That's good luck.*

I admit I find this bride too sentimental. Yet if this had been my wedding, I would have hoped for the same, or at least laughed sweetly if Linnea had been the one to point out such luck shining back in our faces. On a wedding day when the rain does not so much fall down as shoots through, who wouldn't reach for a sign of double hope, double luck, double happiness?

But on this day I see, too, a simpler sign. Two arcs. A double story.

POST-MORTEM

Re-Migrations 2008

Why then did we all show up for this shindig? Obligation? Curiosity? Delusion? Hope? Free lunch?

The June sun has returned, shimmering against our necks and behind our knees, the family of the groom, muttering and chuckling, ambling across the plush lawn, out to the cars, getting ready to migrate back to homes made with no help from Old Country fathers. Linnea repeats the story about the dog on the golf course, and her brother laughs his bass engine laugh and repeats: *Not now. I'm drinking.* I laugh, too loudly perhaps, or from too critical a distance, because this groom is not my father, right? This is not my family?

Someone asks what we all wonder. Why did we come?

Because it was not to be missed, I quip.

You are enjoying this too much, the ex-model sister-in-law says to me.

Yes. I came along because I wanted more of the story. So did we all. But I might be forgetting my place. I am revisiting my broken ground, but Linnea and her siblings have reentered their broken home, the man of the hour not just a story but also their own disappointing father, their mother's disappointing husband.

I might be forgetting this is a wedding of inverses and inverted time, which means for the groom's offspring other versions of themselves, the ones they were as children, walk always beside them. I am forgetting about the scorched terrain every disappointing king leaves in his wake and the ways any man's children work their whole lives to remake what has been unmade in their name.

And am I sure this is not my family? I did choose Linnea, as she chose me, so perhaps, twenty years a willing in-law, this is my family. One of my families, as my family is Linnea's other family.

A few days later, when the redheaded surgeon drives Linnea and me to the airport, she will shake her head, remembering her father, not this new groom. *He treated Mom monstrously,* she will say, as she has said before, will always say.

He says he's not drinking anymore, I will say. *Maybe all this love, all these new people willing to love him, all this sweetness could make him change?*

And I will not believe this myself when I say it, but still I will notice her pause, notice her as she may have looked once, in trouble, slumped, alone, caught in the specimen glass of that Chicago phone booth, considering, resolving. Even if her father is able to change, she may not be willing, we may not be willing, I may not be willing. In the end, it's always the king who is presented with the easier choice.

We don't need our wastelands, but sometimes, still, we want something back, a win for the White Sox, or maybe the Cubs, maybe the Holy Blessing of the Double-Breasted Angel, double meanings, double arcs of light, a doubling back to make up for the love lost the first time through. We all want better citizenry; we all want happier sex; we all want other people's weddings to speak back to our own. We want remnants of pomegranate at the Swedish American buffet. We want love to mean the dead lands re-blooming, the hyacinths come back to life. We all want more than we will get.

He wants to make up for thirty years in one day, Linnea will shrug, as she always shrugs.

Not unwilling.

Not willing.

Her sister will drive us on. We will be anxious to make our plane.

POST-TRAUMATIC

These Fragments We Shore 2008

But also, I came back here because of the view. My arid plain. Windowless steel mills. Smoke spume. The ground with its skin scraped away. My rusty, gouged homeland, promising to, failing to, promising to re-green. Who am I here, in these brief hours of return? Who are Linnea and I, in the lands we left in order to become these two weathered bodies, our annihilation less pending than already survived?

The Indiana Toll Road hovers us back, up onto its filigree, and from that height we see the rust-streaked warehouses, the rubbish of broken rooftops, the clamor of semitrucks and empty barges, but also, in the other direction, residential greenery, lives lived—well or not well—under the Skyway. Waste, but also populous, the blast furnace smog also home to swept bungalows and birds winging between the smokestacks, the spires of industrial cathedrals.

It's a mess, but America was made here.

And some of what America made are people like Linnea and me—seen by some, unseen by others, but here we are, showing up at yet another family wedding, beneath the titter of angels who see or don't see, celebrating this newlywed couple, too old to be new. A father who does, after all, seem to want his children back, or some dancing version of children who don't dance, his rendering of his children, not his children themselves, this father who takes two decades to acknowledge that his eldest daughter has a wife, then does so with his fingers wrapped too tightly around this daughter-in-law's wrist, the father-in-law who angers me less for his mistakes than for what he refuses to see.

Here: abandoned construction materials and inorganic waste, capped with yards of clay, then grass. Here: landfill, but also a park. A double story, like new love, like any love, maybe even like Linnea's and my love, if without the track record. Still it's true that anyone's love might last, might not. The past is falling, always falling in our wake. What becomes of us will be made of these fragments we retain, that we use to shore off a past that does not fall away, that forms more deeply into our foundations. No reinvention without also history.

What is that sound? Apocalypse, Darling? Or our living bodies singing against these necessary ruins?

WHAT'S PRESENT IN TIME FUTURE III

Chicago 2015

The future barely contained in this time past is the father's late marriage that will fail within four seasons, is a resurgent terrain not redeemed but partially remediated in a dailiness of city plans and neighborhood projects, elevated parks and protest marches, new cities made in the wake of the old, that the daughter-in-law will not see until they, this bridegroom's eldest and most not-daughterly daughter and this longtime, newly seen spouse, take new jobs and move back to old Chicago, shifting from the background to the fray, where they re-find the land as they re-found the father, much as always but also with a few sweet hollows of respite, clearings of memory, desire, imperfect, threatened, out of which this stony rubbish might bloom.

But not yet.

POST-PHOTOGRAPHIC

The Photographer's Reformation 2008

Before we leave the golf course, the wedding photographer arranges the crowd, hiding Linnea and me in the back row of the family portrait, as we have both been hidden in back rows of every group since class pictures in grade school—but not because we are lesbians, only because we are tall. The group is large, fifty people. Everyone is present—the ones who'd never left the Old Countries and all the returnees from the new. Squirming children. The broad and mostly middle-aged citizenry of a compound family. The smiling, senior bride and groom, the little bride's arm crooked so her tall new husband can hold her hand. This could be any smallish, living room wedding of high school sweethearts, the bride and groom, anointed harbingers of a long and satisfied future (the role weddings demand of any bride, any groom). This could be the portrait of any wedding, or at least any in which the newlyweds are among the oldest in the room.

What we're talking about here is a wedding that is as much about the past as the future, and we, the wedding guests, are not headless, not turned away, not angels but human, every breathing corpus in the frame—whether believing this bride and her groom married too soon, too late, or just in time—possessing the compressed, sharp juice of memory created within and beyond our families. If held in the palms, split apart with the thumbs, the sweet and disappointing pebbles of anybody's past, fountaining out, staining fingers and pressed wedding skirts and pants, would set the story of any wedding asunder.

We all know this, at this wedding, at any wedding. We all respect the presiding rules of conduct. We smile for the flash. Where there is an old landfill there is also a new golf course. Where there is a wedding vow there may not be any, or there may be just one, or many, rainbows of happiness. Weddings claim to be promises but can never be more than prayers. Where there is a wasteland there may or may not be a resurrection. So once more now. Smile. Look into the camera.

Say PEACE.

POST-INDUSTRIAL DUNES

Memory and Desire 1976 and Now

But before the journey reverses and we return to the Skyway, the siblings already crossing back over, first Linnea and I drive out to the Dunes.

Where the sun is setting and the wind is warm and hard.

Washingnnn.

More than thirty years before, there was such wet darkness here, dead fish belly up in the wake of the waves.

This was when a blond Slav American teenager and the boy she'd been dating for just a few weeks walked this wasteland. She would continue to date this boy just a few weeks more, a tall boy for his age, his parents Mexican immigrants, his father a steelworker, her parents the schoolteacher descendants of city sanitation and mill employees. One of the teenagers is olive-skinned, one brown-skinned, both of them products of those waves of human migration into the smokestack cities of America. They stepped over the poor dead fish, didn't see or smell the stacks because steel mills were for them, then, too familiar to see or smell. They got a little bit high on the joint he pulled out of his pocket, kissed a little bit, but she did not feel the blast furnace of wanting she so wanted to feel, because he was so good-looking, because she was sure it was time, sure she had such a furnace inside her. But this boy and this girl were not on fire for each other, and so they gave up, drove back from Indiana, back to lives that would become, within just a few weeks, expanses across which neither of them would ever again be able to see.

Some other teenagers, another intersection of youth—thirty, forty, fifty years later—will walk where we walked then, and maybe they will make something of this shared ground.

It is to this beach, now a clean beach, that Linnea and I return. Where I return. Linnea has not been here before. We stand in the sand in our wedding guest clothes. Her powder blue shirt rustles and my dress blows up around my knees. Around us middle-aged straight couples in sweat pants and T-shirts gather with lawn chairs. It is a Saturday night in June and the lake gulls career over the waves and children dig in the sand, filling plastic buckets and dumping them out again. Back in the cities the LGBTQ Pride festivals are gathering, but we will miss them this year. The Dunes park rangers set up for a star-gazing session, lessons for the kids, to begin later, after the sun goes down. The rain has cleared, the sky is ruffled with clouds, and the sunset promises to be worth the wait, a slanting gyre across this Great Lakes surf.

To my right, in the far distance, I make out the steam blasts from the Michigan City power plant stacks. To my left smoke flutters from the harbor mill spouts.

I cannot believe this beach will ever be as clean as it seems. I cannot believe disappointing fathers will fully recover lost children. I cannot believe our new country can marry the old one we left, and yet I know these are the only fragments we have, the only shore, the only ruins. O gull. O blowing, shifting dune. O smoking pillars. Bellowing, throat full of fire.

I do not raise my palms, do not block out the stacks. I take Linnea's hand. The lake wind blows my skirt up around my bare knees again as I try to contain everything we've lost and have been given.

NOTES ON THE TEXT

Certainly it is apparent that I have, in this work, borrowed from and expanded upon the language, tone, and structure of T. S. Eliot's long-poem sequence *The Waste Land*. What may not be as clear is that my first pull was the place, not the poem. However, the place has, for me, long evoked the poem, and my explorations of the poem led me, unexpectedly, to re-see the place. Though I did consult scholarly works, my primary method was, over several months, to repeatedly read and hear the poem itself. (I listened to digitized tapes of Eliot's spooky voice—as if he were himself one of the quavering dead crossing London Bridge—as well as to the pearly perfection of a BBC radio reading by the actor John Gielgud.) I was frequently engaged in other activities while listening, most often walking my dogs, until I had assimilated the work as music as well as language.

Mary Karr's essay "How to Read *The Waste Land* So It Alters Your Soul Rather than Just Addling Your Head" (in the Modern Library's edition of *The Waste Land and Other Writings*) helped me in this way of reading, because she suggests readers let this poem "spray in your face, then wash over you" (xxi). Ralph Ellison's passage from his essay collection *Shadow and Act* (excerpted in The Norton Critical Edition of *The Waste Land*)—in which he describes the poem's "discontinuities, its changes of pace, and its hidden system of organization" (166) as a form of jazz—was another of my guides.

Some words I borrowed from Eliot may require definition. *Laquearia* is a light-filled dome or ceiling. In his notes Eliot quotes a passage from Virgil's *Aeneid* which refers to burning torches and gold-paneled ceilings, but in his poem the image conveys the emotional texture of an opulent, over-perfumed interior parlor illuminated by reflected candle flames. *Shantih* ("peace"; also spelled *shanti*) is from a Hindi mantra, calling for tranquility, calm mind and environment, and removal of obstacles. While I am not familiar with the exact constitution of the shanti mantras of Hindu spiritual practice, I understand (or perhaps choose to understand, to meet my convenience) *Shantih shantih shantih* as not unlike the concluding rite of a ritual I did grow up with, the post–Vatican II Catholic mass, where the priest recites, *The Lord Is with You,* the congregation responds, *And Also with You,* and the priest concludes, *The Mass Is Ended. Go in Peace.*

Also a bit of mapping may be in order. The Calumet Region is, according to the understanding of most Chicagoans who know the far South Side, an industrial stretch with no precise borders, running along the South Shore of Lake Michigan (not to be confused with the related—in terms of the relationship of mining to steelmaking—but very differently located Upper Peninsula Michigan copper mining community of Calumet). Chicago's Calumet Region surrounds Lake Calumet and the Calumet River, crosses the Illinois/Indiana border, and is defined and dominated by steel and other heavy industries. U.S. Steel is still one of the major steel producers of the region and once maintained both Gary Works and—on the southeast side of Chicago, near my family's old neighborhood—South Works. But, after the decline of the U.S. steel industry in the 1980s, South Works shut down and the mill was demolished. The 530-acre site was slated for mixed residential and retail development, but after the developers lost their bid for the Obama Presidential Library their plans fell through and the remediated space is now restored prairie built over the former mills—green space except for the remaining ore walls rising from the grass like broken pyramids, too expensive to remove.

Sources citing the steel industry as a leading purveyor of industrial pollution in the Great Lakes Basin are too numerous to list here, and while the area itself is not as well-known as other capitals of industrial pollution (so much so that I often find myself correcting outsiders on the regional pronunciation of the name, which is *CAL-YOU-MET*), no one I grew up with would be surprised to learn that the Calumet Region has often been included on lists of the worst environmental disaster areas on earth. At the same time, organizations such as the Southeast Environmental Task Force are working to promote environmental restoration. In fact, the Indiana Dunes National Lakeshore names the Lake Michigan sand dunes as the birthplace of American ecology, due to writings on the area's plant life by late nineteenth-century University of Chicago botanist Henry Cowles. Jens Jenson, the landscape architect who created many of Chicago's famous parks, dedicated much of his professional life to saving the Indiana Dunes.

Historians and geographers disagree as to the origins of the word *calumet*. Definitions include "ship that draws water" and "deep, still water," according to Indiana author Kenneth Schoon in his book *Calumet Beginnings* (1–2). But the most common definition credits the French spelling of the American Indian name for the river, assumed to refer to the ceremonial pipe used by many Native American tribes (including the Illini, a tribe now missing from the Illinois terrain, except in the remaining caricatures of the University of Illinois intercollegiate team symbol finally deemed hostile and abusive by the NCAA) to convey prayers, or as the concluding rites of peace treaty negotiations. This means the word *calumet* may serve (again, to meet my convenience) as another imprecise metaphor for peace. While repeating this word three times—*Calumet Calumet Calumet*—may not carry the same tranquil music conveyed by the word *Shantih*, perhaps, like parks and golf courses built over piles of dumped slag, the peace of actuality can't help containing the uneven tones and longing of an awkward history.

So *Calumet.*

Cal-you-met.

Cal. You. Met.

ACKNOWLEDGMENTS

I am grateful to everyone at the Rainier Writing Workshop, then and now, for their part in the creation of a place, time, and way of being that allowed me to conceive of this book. Thanks to the *Seneca Review* and *The Ocean State Review* for publishing portions of the book and to editors Jen Hirt and Erin Murphy for reprinting the first excerpt in the SUNY University Press anthology *Creating Nonfiction*. Thank you to my agent, Malaga Baldi, and more thanks to Kristen Elias Rowley and Joy Castro for creating Machete: The Ohio State Series in Literary Nonfiction to make space for unconventional nonfiction by diverse writers, and for their fierce embrace of the latest iteration of this manuscript, and thanks to all the editors, designers, and publicists at Mad Creek Books of the Ohio State University Press for their hard work on this manuscript. Thanks to photographer and Chicago far South Side native Laura Migliorino for the cover photograph as well as for her stunning frontispiece image from the Calumet Region. As always, I thank family—the people who made me as well as the people who made my spouse Linnea—for putting up with a creative nonfiction writer in their midst. I will never be able to thank Linnea enough for the steadfast support and willingness to let me put the work first in our life together. Although they knew no other way of living, I thank the now departed Miss Dusty Springfield and Miss Rosemary Clooney for their curly canine companionship as I worked. And thanks to 250 square feet in the Calhoun Building at LynLake in Minneapolis—my urban retreat and for many years my do-it-yourself writing residency— for the creative sanctuary of the wee hours and some of the best and most focused writing time I've experienced in my life. And finally, my deepest thanks to Judith Kitchen, for her tireless, passionate, fluent, and fully comprehending support of this project from its inception. I wish she had lived to see the book in print.

ABOUT THE AUTHOR

Barrie Jean Borich grew up in Riverdale and South Holland, just south of the Chicago city line in the Calumet Region, and both her parents grew up in the industrial neighborhoods of Southeast Chicago. She is the author of *Body Geographic* (University of Nebraska Press/American Lives Series) which won a Lambda Literary Award in Memoir and an IPPY (Independent Publisher Book Award) Gold Medal in Essay/Creative Nonfiction. Her book *My Lesbian Husband* (Graywolf) won the American Library Association Stonewall Book Award, and her work has been cited in *Best American Essays* and *Best American Nonrequired Reading*. Borich is an associate professor in the Department of English and the MA in Writing and Publishing Program at DePaul University in Chicago, where she edits *Slag Glass City*, a digital journal of the urban essay arts. Though a South Sider by blood, Borich lives with her spouse Linnea on the North Side of Chicago, in the Bryn Mawr Historic District of the Edgewater Beach neighborhood.

ALSO BY THIS AUTHOR

Restoring the Color of Roses
My Lesbian Husband
Body Geographic